The Landscape of the Cotsw

The Landscape of the Cotswolds

AMBASSADOR

SALMON

Published by J Salmon Limited
100 London Road, Sevenoaks, Kent TN13 1BB

First edition 1999
Second edition 2001
Third edition 2003

Designed by the Salmon Studio

Copyright © 2003 J Salmon Limited

ISBN 1 898435 84 7

Printed in England by
J Salmon Limited, Tubs Hill Works, Sevenoaks, Kent

Front cover: Arlington Row, Bibury
Back cover: A cottage window, Duntisbourne Leer
Half title page: A Cotswold lane
Title page: Blockley

The Post Office, Great Tew

Introduction

The Cotswolds lie in the very heart of England and, for travellers, can be reached from towns and cities which are themselves well worthy of their time and attention: in the west from Cheltenham, genteel spa town of Regency terraces and arcades, in the north from Stratford-upon-Avon, redolent with the atmosphere of the immortal Bard, or in the south from Bath, the Aquae Sulis of Roman times. But for an introduction to the beauties of the region there is surely no better approach than from Oxford, city of dreaming spires, past Witney and up the valleys either of the Coln, through beautiful Bibury, or the Windrush to Burford and Bourton-on-the-Water, the Venice of the Cotswolds.

The Cotswold hills form a solid limestone ridge between the orchards and pastures of Worcestershire and the valley of the Thames, and extend about sixty miles, from the borders of Wiltshire in the south-west to Shakespeare's Avon in the north-east. While they only twice exceed the 1,000 foot level, at Cleeve Hill and Broadway Tower, the escarpment, overlooking the Severn valley, maintains a fairly consistent eight hundred feet. The scenery that clothes these hills has an individual character that had impressed itself on men's minds before Shakespeare wrote of its 'high wild hills'. Its atmosphere has an intangible but very pervasive quality which is hard to analyse but has some connection with the various elements that go to make up the Cotswold picture: the spacious beauty of the wolds intermingled with beech woodland etched against a broad sky, and the seclusion of the valleys with their pollarded willows and clear streams threading a string of villages built in the honey-coloured local stone.

It was sheep that brought prosperity to these Cotswold valleys. The first wealth came to the medieval wool merchants, whose pack-trains wound their way across England from Chipping Campden, Northleach, Cirencester and other centres, loaded with material for Europe. Wool halls were built in the towns for storage and distribution; fine houses sprang up for the staplers, cottages for their workers and a vernacular style architecture was born. Merchants of the status of William Grevel of Chipping Campden, who died in 1401, had trade connections extending over half Europe.

The 'Cotswold style' of architecture seems to date from the close of the fourteenth century; certainly by the fifteenth and sixteenth it had reached its zenith in buildings such as Grevel's House at Chipping Campden and Icomb Manor, which were well ahead of their time. Here one has the unmistakable characteristics of the next two centuries, with the solid dignity of gable and chimney, stone-mullioned windows grouped in tiers and an occasional projecting bay or oriel. The houses, like the churches, and even the barns, were roofed with the stone slates that weather so exquisitely. Even groups of labourers' cottages, such as little Arlington Row at Bibury, seem to exude something of the same air, though it is the smaller manor-houses and rich town dwellings that are the supreme Cotswold products. The examples of this at Owlpen, Upper Swell, Upper Slaughter, Snowshill, and a dozen more in towns and villages throughout Gloucestershire are certainly worthy of all the high praise bestowed upon them.

A word must also be said of the churches. The beginnings of prosperity in the thirteenth century are reflected in an Early English group; North Cerney and the Duntisbournes are particularly attractive, with their saddleback towers. But the glory of the district is its later 'wool' churches that, collectively, remain as grand a memorial to the generosity of their merchant benefactors as to the genius of the masons who evolved such splendours from the resources of the local stone. Buildings such as the Cirencester, Northleach, Winchcombe, Fairford and Chipping Campden churches can rank with any in the country in their beauty of craftsmanship. No visitor to Cotswold can afford to miss them.

Winter at Broadway Tower ▷

The beautiful and dignified old town of **Burford** in Oxfordshire was the site of a fortified ford over the River Windrush in Anglo-Saxon times and the town grew to be an important crossroads where the north-south route met the east-west. Numerous coaching inns sprang up to meet the needs of travellers and the strong local tradition of building has produced, over the years, charming houses and inns of seemingly endless variety. The wide, grass-bordered main street runs down to the peaceful River Windrush and half way down the street is the Tolsey, an old pillared customs house which now contains a local museum. The Parish Church is an impressive building, dating from Norman times but with many later additions. Almshouses founded in 1457 adjoin the churchyard and throughout the town there are many charming cottages which appear virtually unchanged since Tudor times.

◁ Cottages at Burford
River Windrush at Burford ▷

Situated in the pretty valley of the River Windrush not far from Burford, the village of **Swinbrook** is known for its tiny church where effigies of the Fettiplace family, who owned the village for generations, are arranged on shelves on the chancel wall. So sheltered is the village that in medieval times a vineyard flourished nearby. Swinbrook House was built by the second Lord Redesdale and in the 1920s it was the home of his large family which included the writers Jessica and Nancy Mitford. The extensive gardens include lawns interspersed with luxuriant herbaceous plants as well as a colourful rose border. A few miles to the east is **Witney**, a bustling little town on the edge of the Cotswolds. The weaving of woollen cloth is believed to have begun here in Roman times and Witney became famous for the production of fine blankets. Among many historically interesting buildings in the town is the Blanket Hall, erected in 1721, where blankets were brought to be weighed and measured. A pleasant green extends from the Buttercross, at the top of the main street, to the ancient church at the southern end of the town.

◁ Swinbrook Gardens
The Buttercross, Witney ▷

Facing each other across the River Leach and linked by an ancient clapper bridge, the twin hamlets of Eastleach Turville and **Eastleach Martin** in Gloucestershire date from Norman times. There are a number of charming old Cotswold cottages in Eastleach Martin as well as some 19th century almshouses and ancient farmsteads. The Church of St. Michael and St. Martin boasts five ancient sundials and contains some beautiful Norman and 14th century work. Another interesting church is found at **Broadwell** in Oxfordshire. It stands at the end of Dead Man's Lane down which funeral processions came from outlying parts of the parish. Standing almost within the churchyard is a delightful thatched cottage which may originally have housed the parson. The shaft is all that remains of a medieval cross which also stands near the church.

◁ The Parish Church, Broadwell
Eastleach Martin ▷

The farming community of **Kelmscot** lies east of Lechlade on the southern edge of the Cotswolds. The village is closely associated with the 19th century artist and poet William Morris who lived here for 25 years and named his London printing press after the village. He shared Elizabethan Kelmscott Manor for a time with Rossetti and this fine Cotswold stone house has now been restored as a Morris museum. William Morris is buried in a family tomb in the churchyard of St. George's Church in Kelmscot and the group of cottages which stands near the church was built in 1902 by his widow as a memorial to him. Across the River Thames in Berkshire is Buscot, an interesting village where the stone-built estate cottages were influenced by William Morris's ideas and built by the Butler-Henderson family who played an important part in the development of the railways. **Buscot Lock** is popular with holiday-makers on the river. The original pound lock was built in 1790 and beside it stands an attractive stone cottage where the resident lock-keeper lived.

◁ Buscot Lock
Kelmscott Manor ▷

The 19th century artist and poet William Morris called **Bibury** "the most beautiful village in England". It nestles in the valley of the River Coln and, with its partly Saxon church, 17th century mill and cottages of Cotswold stone it is the epitome of the English countryside. The delightful terrace known as Arlington Row was originally built in the 14th century as a sheephouse. Later, in the 1600s, it was converted to house the weavers who supplied cloth to nearby Arlington Mill which today houses a museum containing furniture from the Cotswolds Arts and Crafts movement. The mill-stream runs into the trout-filled River Coln which flows between the Mill House and the creeper-hung Swan Hotel. Here it is crossed by a handsome bridge dating from 1770. In the centre of the village, the square is overlooked by St. Mary's Church. Much of the original Saxon work is still in evidence although the church has many Norman and medieval additions.

◁ Arlington Row, Bibury
River Coln, Bibury ▷

Duntisbourne Leer is one of a group of three Gloucestershire villages situated in the valley of the little River Dun on the southern edge of the Cotswolds. At one time it belonged to the abbey of Lire in Normandy, hence the second part of the name. **North Cerney** is a pretty Cotswold village in the Churn valley. The church, which retains some Norman features although it was largely rebuilt in the 1470s following a fire, attracts a great deal of interest. It displays an intriguing saddle-back tower as well as a fine carved stone pulpit. A typical Cotswold feature is the window, now blocked, above the chancel arch. In the churchyard there is a well-restored 14th century cross.

◁ Cottage window at Duntisbourne Leer
A winter's day, North Cerney ▷

Known as the "capital of the Cotswolds", and an excellent touring centre, **Cirencester** is rich in history, successfully blending modern buildings with dignified old houses of Cotswold stone. The second largest town in Britain under the Romans, Cirencester became an important wool market in medieval times and it is from this period that the magnificent Church of St. John the Baptist dates. Overlooking the busy Market Place, it is one of the longest parish churches in England with a soaring west tower and a unique three-storied south porch, built by the guilds in 1500. Among many features of interest inside the church are wall-paintings, some remarkable fan vaulting and a pulpit of 1515 which is in the 'wine-glass' shape common to many Gloucestershire churches. **Northleach**, set on high ground between the valleys of the Coln and Windrush rivers, also grew rich in the 15th century from the wool trade. This prosperity resulted in the building of the impressive church with its battlemented and pinnacled roof and beautiful south porch. Rich in memorials to the great wool merchants, the church also rewards the attentive visitor with features such as 12th century builders' marks and a delightful 14th century font where the bowl is supported by angels while the base stands upon the evil spirits.

◁ The Parish Church, Cirencester
The Parish Church, Northleach ▷

Sometimes called "Queen of the Cotswolds" **Painswick** is one of the most interesting of the wool towns and is full of quaint corners and picturesque streets. It was visited by both Henry VIII and Charles I and the beautiful 15th century church was the scene of a Civil War skirmish. In the churchyard stand the famous clipped yew trees, traditionally said to be 99 in number, some of which are more than 200 years old. **Minchinhampton** is now a tranquil south Cotswold country town but once it was a thriving centre of the textile industry. The fine Market Hall of 1698 is a reminder of busier days. Holy Trinity Church has an unusual short steeple, or octagonal tower, decorated with pinnacles which were added during restoration by the Victorians. Minchinhampton Common, owned by the National Trust, has yielded many fossils and gives superb views over Stroud and the Golden Valley.

◁ An old corner, Painswick
The Market Hall, Minchinhampton ▷

On high ground just south of Stroud, **Rodborough Common** offers splendid views of the River Frome valley. Rodborough Fort, a fine castellated mansion with no military significance, built on the northern edge of the common. In the delightful hamlet of **Owlpen** stands a delightful manor house of 15th century origin. Overlooked by the fine Cotswold stone church and set amid 16th and 17th century formal terraced gardens, this splendid manor includes a barn, a mill and a court house. The house contains unique painted cloth wall hangings. It was here that King Henry VI's wife, Margaret of Anjou, stayed before the Battle of Tewkesbury and it is said that she still haunts the Great Chamber.

◁ Rodborough Fort
Owlpen Manor ▷

Photograph copyright J. Cull

With its wide streets and interesting old buildings, **Tetbury** is a picturesque market town with a long history. Roman and Saxon remains have been found in the area and the church dates from Norman times although it was re-built in the 18th century with the conspicuous spire and tower being reconstructed in 1890. For centuries Tetbury was a flourishing centre of the wool trade as some fine houses built by prosperous merchants testify. In the centre of the town stands the splendid pillared Market Hall, a traditional feature of many old wool towns. Now used as a Town Hall, the building dates from Elizabethan times.

◁ Westonbirt Arboretum
Market Hall, Tetbury ▷

A beautifully planned town graced by dignified Regency architecture and spacious tree-lined avenues, **Cheltenham** has a peaceful charm reminiscent of an earlier age. The town developed as a spa after the first medicinal spring was discovered in the early 18th century and it became fashionable after King George III took the waters here in 1788. Later the Duke of Wellington was also an advocate of the curative powers of the waters. The Pittville Pump Room is an outstanding example of Regency architecture. This fine domed and colonnaded building was built for Joseph Pitt MP in the late 1820s and is set in a spacious park with lakes and sweeping lawns. Among Cheltenham's other outstanding architectural features is the fine terrace which lines the Promenade and incorporates the municipal offices. Situated in the heart of the Cotswolds, Cheltenham is renowned throughout the world for its festivals of music and literature and the appeal of this elegant resort is enhanced by many colourful gardens which offer a peaceful respite from the bustle of daily life.

◁ Pittville Spa, Cheltenham
The Promenade, Cheltenham ▷

Once a walled town of some importance, the history of **Winchcombe** goes back to the 8th century when the great abbey, now vanished, was founded. A number of imposing houses which were built in the prosperous years still stand but today Winchcombe is a quiet little village sheltering in a well-wooded valley. It has many pretty cottages such as these in Vineyard Street which are picturesquely built in local Gloucestershire stone. Situated not far from Winchcombe, 15th century **Sudeley Castle** is surrounded by delightful gardens. They include a fine formal flower garden and a topiary garden with splendid 15 feet high yew hedges. The castle has many connections with royalty and Catherine Parr, sixth wife of Henry VIII, is buried here.

◁ Sudeley Castle
Vineyard Street, Winchcombe ▷

Some three miles apart in the valley of the beautiful River Windrush are two outstanding Cotswold villages: Naunton and Guiting Power. **Naunton**, situated at the foot of the hills, provides a typical Cotswold scene. Houses and cottages of mellow local stone help to preserve the rural character of the village and the church contains a number of interesting monuments, some relating to the Civil War. **Guiting Power** possesses a handful of attactive stone-built cottages, their irregular roofs, chimneys and gables standing at angles to each other offering a memorable picture. They look out on to a triangular village green where the War Memorial has the appearance of a medieval cross. On a knoll beside the river stands the fine restored church which has some notable Norman doorways.

◁ Wintertime, Naunton
The Cross, Guiting Power ▷

Centred on the gentle slopes of the Cotswold Hills, this beautiful area can proudly claim to be the most unspoilt part of the English countryside. Its scores of hamlets and villages nestling into the folds of the wolds are all built of the local limestone of a warm yellow colour that has been saturated with the sun of centuries. They are so much in harmony with their surroundings that they give the impression of having grown almost naturally out of each hillside. One of the most delightful of all these villages, **Upper Slaughter** stands on a grassy slope above the stream. It possesses a fine gabled manor house parts of which date back to the 15th century as well as a number of the attractive old stone cottages which are typical of the area. Upper Slaughter is also known for its fine Norman church. It boasts two fonts, one of which dates from the 15th century, and an outstanding arch with some exceptionally well-preserved moulding.

◁ On the Cotswold hills
The Parish Church, Upper Slaughter ▷

Joined to its twin village of Upper Slaughter by the little River Eye, **Lower Slaughter** is redolent with all the character and charm of the Cotswolds. Nestling in the shelter of the hills, the village was once an administrative centre of some importance and a court was held here from the Middle Ages until the 17th century. The main street and the square are notable for the impressive buildings which line them, Manor Farm, enlarged in 1688; the mid-17th century Manor House; the old corn-mill and numerous delightful stone cottages. St, Mary's Church was largely re-built in the Victorian era but stands on medieval foundations. Water is never far away in the Cotswolds and at Lower Slaughter the stream meanders through the centre of the village, crossed by low foot-bridges, some of stone, some of oak planks on stone pillars. Many of the mellow, honey-coloured stone cottages were built by their eventual tenants, using a site and materials provided by the landlord. The stone tile quarries in the area have been worked since Roman times and it is the use of local materials which gives to villages like Lower Slaughter their appealing sense of unity.

◁ Lower Slaughter ▷

With its tree-shaded green, riverside paths and honey-coloured buildings in secluded lanes, **Bourton-on-the-Water** is a favourite spot for visitors to the Cotswolds. It is often referred to as the Venice of the Cotswolds on account of the elegant stone bridges which span the crystal clear waters of the River Windrush as it flows through the centre of the village. Two of these date from the 18th century and the Old Mill Bridge stands near an 18th century corn-mill which now houses a museum. As well as its mellow architecture, Bourton contains a number of attractions including a model village and a botanical garden. The village is a good centre for walks and many roads ascend the hills, offering glorious views across the valley with its little villages and ancient farmsteads tucked into sheltered corners.

◁ River Windrush at Bourton-on-the-Water ▷

The small but thriving market town of **Moreton-in-Marsh** has grown up along the line of the Roman Fosse Way on the northern edge of the Cotswolds. The stately Market Hall stands prominently in the middle of its broad tree-lined main street beyond a small green where a market is still held to this day. The village stocks stand on the green and nearby is the medieval Curfew Tower which is one of the oldest buildings in Moreton. It still contains the original curfew bell which was tolled each night until 1860. Also standing on the Fosse Way, **Stow-on-the-Wold** is situated at the junction of seven main routes. It was for many centuries a prominent trading centre, famous for its great annual sheep fairs, and the vast market square still testifies to the original importance of the town. With its stocks and old cross, the square is protected from the winds which sweep across the wolds by the ancient houses and inns which surround it.

◁ Moreton-in-Marsh
The Stocks, Stow-on-the-Wold ▷

One of the prettiest villages around the northern edge of the Cotswolds, **Stanton** nestles beneath Shenbarrow Hill. It has an attractive main street and a number of delightful corners where the ancient houses are built in typical Cotswold style with steeply-pitched gables, mullioned casements and glowing stone walls. That they present much the same appearance as when they were built around 1600, is largely due to sympathetic restoration by the architect Sir Philip Scott in the early 1900s. There is much of historical interest in the splendid Parish Church of St. Michael and All Angels. Some medieval pews have survived and there is evidence that prisoners were housed here during the Civil War. Work by 20th century architect Sir Ninian Comper on the rood screen, organ loft and some of the windows was sympathetic to the church's Norman origins. He was also responsible for restoring the medieval cross which stands by a row of charming cottages. Situated on the ancient Stane Way which gave the village its name, **Stanway** is known for its fine 17th century hall, which has a splendid gabled gatehouse, and for its magnificent tithe barn. The church has been much restored but it was originally a dignified Norman building and retains a number of Norman carvings around the chancel walls. A number of picturesque thatched cottages are found in or near this small village, epitomising the peaceful charm for which the area is famous.

◁ The Parish Chuch, Stanton
The Gatehouse, Stanway ▷

Nestling beneath wooded slopes, the little village of **Blockley** is clustered around its handsome church, the tower of which was rebuilt after a great storm in 1703. It retains a Norman door and some interesting monuments. Many of the picturesque stone cottages were originally mill-workers houses and the streams which now flow peacefully through the valley once turned mill-wheels. The remote but beautiful hamlet of **Snowshill** is superbly situated in a narrow upland valley, surrounded by open country which was once owned by St. Mary's Abbey at Winchcombe. Some typical Cotswold cottages are clustered around a triangular green near the Church of St. Barnabas which was almost entirely rebuilt in 1864. A delightful Tudor manor house, now cared for by the National Trust, houses a collection of ancient crafts including clocks, toys and tools.

◁ Blockley
Snowshill ▷

Broadway in Worcestershire is deservedly one of the most famous of all Cotswold villages with its wealth of mellow stone houses and picturesque old inns, many of them dating from the 16th and 17th centuries and some, like the outstanding group of cottages in Bankside, from the 15th. The Lygon Arms was once a coaching inn where both Charles I and Oliver Cromwell stayed and in the 19th century the town was frequented by many famous writers and artists. The wide main street slopes gently up from the attractive green where an ancient edict still permits an annual fair to be held. From Broadway Tower, a fortress-like folly which was built in 1800 on a nearby 1,024 feet high hill, there are magnificent views in all directions which encompass not only the Cotswold Hills but also the Vale of Evesham, the distant ridge of the Malverns and the Forest of Dean.

◁ High Street, Broadway
Wistaria Cottage, Broadway ▷

Surrounded by farms and market gardens, **Childswickham** lies near Broadway where the Cotswolds begin to give way to the Vale of Evesham. Much of the old-world charm of the village is preserved in its rich variety of architecture. Cottages of honey-coloured stone are contrasted with weathered brick and half-timbered home-steads while the Norman parish church has a slender 15th century spire. The original top of the village cross was destroyed by the Puritans and later replaced by an urn from the churchyard. To the north-east, beyond Chipping Campden is secluded **Hidcote Bartrim**, surrounded by wooded countryside and winding lanes. Best known for the famous gardens at Hidcote Manor, the hamlet also has some delightful thatched cottages.

◁ The Cross, Childswickham
Cottages at Hidcote Bartrim ▷

Hidcote Manor lies on the leafy borders of Gloucestershire and Warwickshire in the heart of rural England, but within easy reach of both Broadway and Chipping Campden. The house itself is an unpretentious Cotswold manor with a chapel to one side of the courtyard. It is for its magnificent gardens, however, that Hidcote is best known. They were created by horticulturalist Major Lawrence Johnston when he acquired the estate in 1905 and are a permanent monument to his vision since what is now Hidcote Manor Garden was then simply fields with a few trees. Now owned by the National Trust the garden comprises a series of delightful small areas each surrounded by walls or variegated hedges and devoted to one species or colour combination.

◁ Hidcote Manor Gardens
   Hidcote Manor ▷

A mile from Broadway on the road to Chipping Campden lies the pretty little village of **Willersey** with its picturesque Bell Inn and a number of old cottages grouped around the green and duck-pond. The church is mainly early-English in origin and its six bells were re-cast in 1712 from the original three. The name "chipping", which is found in several Cotswold towns, is derived from the old English word for market and **Chipping Campden** was a prosperous centre of the medieval wool trade. The splendid Jacobean Market Hall with its pointed gables and graceful arches dates from 1627. One of the jewels of the Cotswolds, the town is famous for its dignified mellowed stone architecture and the graceful curving High Street has been described as "the most beautiful village street in England". St. James's Church dates from the 15th century and it contains many splendid brasses and some priceless examples of medieval embroidered work. Nearby stand some fine 17th century almshouses endowed by the first Viscount Campden who was also responsible for building a fine mansion to the south of the church. This was largely destroyed during the Civil War but the gateway, pavilions and almonry which remain give an indication of the magnificence of the original house.

◁ The Pond, Willersey

Campden Manor and Church, Chipping Campden ▷

Although it lies just beyond the northern edge ot the Cotswolds, the Warwickshire village of **Ilmington** is an archetypal Cotswold village of mellow stone cottages with lichen-covered roofs and mullioned windows. The two greens, upper and lower, are overlooked by cottages, inns and a Norman church, and the splendid Manor House was built in the 16th century. A few miles to the south-east is **Long Compton**, another remarkable old village which is overlooked by the ancient stone circle known as the Rollright Stones. Alongside Long Compton's thatched stone cottages and medieval cross, now serving as a drinking fountain, stands the Church of St. Peter and St. Paul. It dates from the 13th century and has an intriguing lych-gate which is built in the style of a thatched cottage with the ground floor removed. The room which remains above the archway is used to house a village museum.

◁ Ilmington Manor
The Lych-gate, Long Compton ▷

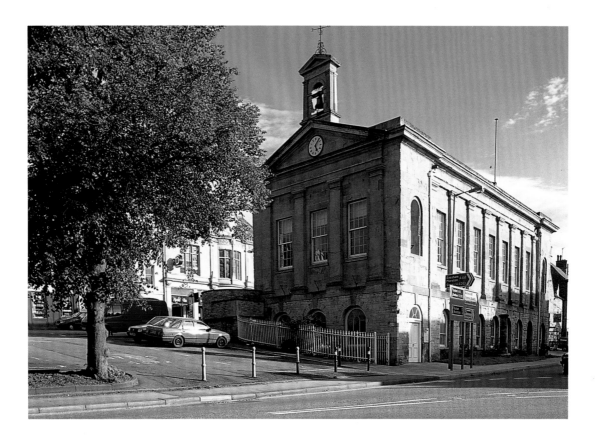

Another of the Cotswolds' medieval market towns, **Chipping Norton** has the distinction of being the highest town in Oxfordshire at 700 feet. The parish church is noted for its fine chancel and has some interesting tombs and monumental brasses while ancient coaching inns, stone-built houses and attractive almshouses add to the appeal of this beautiful little town. Among its many fine buildings is the Town Hall, built in the classical style, which stands at one end of the market place. Set on a lofty ridge of the Cotswold hills not far from the town is the ancient stone circle known as the **Rollright Stones.** It consists of two groups of stones, the King's Men and the Whispering Knights. Standing apart, on the other side of the road, is the solitary King Stone. Local folklore suggests that the stones represent a would-be conqueror of England who was turned into stone by a witch along with his army and a group of dissident knights.

◁ Town Hall, Chipping Norton
Rollright Stones ▷

Lying in a hollow of the Cotswold hills, **Great Tew** is one of England's prettiest villages. Facing the tree-shaded green, a row of thatched cottages stands beside the 18th century, stone-roofed Falkland Arms Inn. A Victorian school house stands on the other side of the green and in the Norman church, on a hillside away from the village, there are some interesting monuments and brasses. The appearance of the village owes much to a young Scot, John Claudius Loudon, who was in charge of the estate in the late 18th and early 19th centuries. He resisted the fashion for replacing or moving estate cottages and ensured that many of these picturesque homes were sensitively preserved. The numerous evergreens throughout the village and the neat box hedges also resulted from his influence.

◁ The village street, Great Tew

Cottages at Great Tew ▷

Index